I0548164

Poems
and
Prayers
from the
Soul

Kimberly N. Bennett

Published by

Kimberly N. Bennett

Post Office Box 6

Scotland, MD 20687

angelicbooks@gmail.com

Printed in the United States of America

ISBN   978-0-6151-5835-8

Special Dedications:

I would like to give honor to God,
For all that he has done for me and all
He will do. I want to thank him for choosing
Me! Thanks to my family, and my
Church family for all of your support.
I Love You All!!

IN LOVING MEMORY OF
MY MOMMY... MAE HELEN BENNETT
JUNE 8, 1943 – SEPTEMBER 14, 2006

Opening Prayer

Heavenly Father I come to you in prayer, thanking you for all you have done for me and all you will do! Thank you for allowing me to see a day I've never seen before, having the right state of my mind and the movement of my limbs. Thank you for placing a shield of protection around me and my family. I thank you for all of the blessings you have showered down upon my friends and my enemies. I thank you for your mercy, your guidance and your patience. I pray that I may be more like you as I walk this Christian journey. May your blessings be upon this book and all who read it. Within these pages may they find strength, hope and the realization that they are not alone. While reading this book may they feel your presence, your anointing and your light through my words, for I am your servant doing your will! In Jesus name I pray…Amen!

Taking a Look into My Soul

God had been speaking to me every since I was a young child. I always found myself attending church, and yearning to know more about the Lord. The Holy Spirit has always dwelled inside of me. I began to notice more and more when I was in the 11th or 12th grade that I had a gift. Like most Christians, I found myself going to church all the time and then of course I fell to the ways of the world but I found my way back to the ways of God. We all battle with the ways of the world, those of us who have that spiritual foundation know where we should be, we know what we should be doing, but it is much easier to do what everyone else is doing. It was not until my mother was getting sick around October 2005 that I began to get closer to God. The vision and title for my book "Poems and Prayers from the Soul" came in June 2006 while I was taking a walk. I began to write and I couldn't stop. Day after day God was placing different things in me to let out, and I loved every moment. Writing ones thoughts is the easiest part, creating a book is the hardest but I love to say "With God on your side all things are possible!" Around the time I wrote "Poems and Prayers from the Soul", I wrote two other books and I chose a different one to be published first, but when God has something for you to do he will see that vision through to the end. God said in a still small voice to be obedient. Even though "Poems and Prayers from the Soul" was not completed God had a plan and it was my duty to fulfill it! Through prayer, perseverance, patience and the grace of God I am blessed to lead you into my soul through Poems and Prayers! Thank you for your support and I pray that as you travel through my soul you will find things that you can relate to, things that give you comfort and insight knowing you are not the only one and wisdom to learn from what someone else was delivered from and to see what God can and will do if only you allow him to do all that he needs to with you and your soul!

CONTENTS

Poems from my Soul

Prayers from my Soul

Poems and Prayers from your Soul

Poems from my Soul

Where I've Been and Where I'm Going

I've been many places in my lifetime.

I've seen and experienced many things.

I've been from Maryland to Minnesota and a parent at nineteen.

I've been lied to and mistreated.

I've been lied on and misleaded.

I've accepted Jesus as my savior and then I turned my back on him.

I've been lost, but now I'm found.

I felt like I was drowning in a pool of despair.

I was gasping for air, rethinking all the things I've done over the years.

Recalling exactly Where I've Been

and praying for God to show me Where I'm Going.

When I was about to take what felt like my last breath

I felt a rope being thrown out to save me…It is called "The Word".

And once again the "Life Guard" had saved me!

My "Life Guard" is God!

Where I've Been and Where I'm Going, it's amazing how words could

hold such an in depth meaning. Most would think I am speaking

of places, locations, education or goals. But I am talking about

Where I was, things I've done in my life, the way I've been living. Where
I'm Going is where all Christians and sinners striving to be Christians
dream of one day going. It is what we dream of; it is the vacation of all
vacations! It is the rest we can only imagine of

One day having, it is our last and final trip.

I like to call it our

"ETERNAL VACATIONING SPOT"!

Where I've Been and Where I'm Going...

At the time I didn't feel anything was wrong with the way I was living. But Thanks be to God he had a bigger plan for me and now I am spending the rest of my life living it out.

FEELINGS

Happy yet Sad

Smiling yet Crying

Loving yet Lost

Joyful yet Depressed

These are all the feelings that I have experienced. I have always been a happy, helpful, exciting, talkative kind of person. But often when I was smiling and joyful on the outside I was crying on the inside. I was lost, my body was living, but my soul was dying. I began to doubt God and myself. I often wondered why me, what have I done, when was I such a bad person that I have to suffer and feel like this? Many nights I cried myself to sleep. Many nights I called for God to save me, as I slept he whispered my child one day the pain will not seem so bad and the questions you ask me you will have the answers and the smile you share with others you will feel it the way others do. Then I couldn't imagine understanding why I felt the way I did, but thanks be to God I finally know. God was preparing me for the use of my talents. How can I testify if I've never been at my lowest moment, how can I pray and speak to others about the troubles of the world if I've never been out in the world. God allows us to experience certain things, but he also has instilled in all of us the ability to call out for help. And then and only then will you be able to carry out his work. You have to die before you can live.

FEELINGS ...

When I was experiencing all of these feelings I could not imagine telling anyone. I never thought anyone else in the world felt like me, and I thought no one could possibly understand. But God was patient and he waited for me to call out for help, and when I did

He Saved Me!

BEING...NOT LIVING

It's been a while since I have been moved to write, my life was not my life. Things were happening, time was passing and I was just there...not really living it. Some things I cannot explain, some things I did not retain, and some things I prayed for never came to exist so one day I gave up...no longer to persist. No pushing, no begging, no standing firm on my conquest. I felt no rest...I had forgotten I was blessed! I would weep, I would cry and at times I would wonder why she had to die. My mind wonders, my eyes water, my thoughts drift into mid air...They are no longer there...I am no longer here... Where did I go, when did I leave, how do I get back...To living and not just being? This smile hides so much, my words they often touch...a soul, a mind, a heart, but when will they speak back to me, when will they rebuttal what I have said to so many, when will I digest what I have professed to so many? When will I believe my own words, when will I begin to live instead of just being?

BEING...NOT LIVING...

I wrote this shortly after loosing my mother to cancer and I know there are so many who can relate to what I am saying, so many of us have experienced something that left us feeling empty, left us feeling lost. That is why I felt the need to include this poem to let others know that it is normal to feel lost and to feel far from what you are used to being, but you need to know through prayer and faith, you will be delivered!

PRAYER

The Power of Prayer ...... Prayer can heal,

Prayer can restore, prayer can transform.

The word Prayer holds a real and true meaning!

P is for POWER

R is for RELIABLE

A is for ABILITY

Y is for YEARNING

E is for EXPERT

R is for RATIONALIZE

Through Prayer we all have the **POWER** to call on the only one who is **RELIABLE**. The only one who has the **ABILITY** to satisfy our **YEARNING**. Prayer allows us to call on the **EXPERT**, the only one who is able to **RATIONALIZE** our needs and our wants.

There's so much strength and power in prayer. You can only gain when using prayer, you will never lose!

PRAYER ...

At times the only thing I had left was Prayer! The power of prayer is endless! Prayer can bring healing, comfort and light when all around you is darkness.

Will We Ever Learn

We walk around with our $120 shoes, our $75 pants, our $30 shirts, our $12 socks and our bling and we think we are above the laws. I am not talking about the laws of the world; I am talking about Gods laws.

When God created us we came into the world bare. No clothes on our backs and no shoes on our feet, but one thing that was dressed were our souls!

Will We Ever Learn that clothing doesn't make the person. If our souls are not right with God, it doesn't matter what you have on or how much you had to pay.

God and Christians of the world see you in a different light. It is like you are being looked at through x-rayed glasses, your outer body doesn't matter it's what's going on inside that counts.

Will We Ever Learn that God and Jesus are our instructors they teach us right from wrong and how to get our lives in order.

The question is when will you sign up for the class?

Will We Ever Learn...

We have to realize that God is eternal. There is no end to his existence or his blessings. Our earthly possessions are just that. They will never get us into heaven!

Why Do We Not Listen

Why do we not listen?
Why can't we hear him until it is too late?

Why do we ignore him as if there is hate?

Why do what we know is wrong,
Why do we settle for being weak instead
of striving to be strong?

Why do we worship material things and
curse our saving grace?

Why do we forget all that God has done for us when we should use each moment as a stepping-stone to see his face one day?

Why Do We Not Listen...

God is constantly trying to tell us something, but we're never willing to listen. We need to take time out to ask God what he needs from us and how can we make him proud to be our Father.

ACCEPTING OURSELVES

When we were young we looked for
acceptance in our friends and our classmates.

When we became teenagers we looked for
acceptance in our parents, teachers, and the community.

As adults who have not accepted God we look for
acceptance in our jobs, our boss, our children, and mostly the world.

As a saved child of God we look for
acceptance in God! Accepting God into our lives
and into our hearts will finally result in accepting ourselves!

It is sad and lonely looking at this world full of people
wondering around aimlessly lost, wondering which way to turn,
where to go. People who have no spiritual foundation and who are
looking for acceptance out there and have no
idea that all they need to do is accept God, and then and only
then will they be able to accept themselves!

For so long I was looking for
acceptance in the club, in my friends and in drinks. I know
that I am far from being perfect, but I Thank God for choosing
me, that little girl from the boonies.
When I decided to accept him, I finally accepted myself and who
God had planned for me to be.
I have been blessed with amazing talents and
I refuse to let them be in vain.

Accepting Ourselves ...

When you have a spiritual foundation and God lives in you, it doesn't matter how far you may stray because he is always there. It's hard to accept ourselves because we know we're not living right. We know there's more to life than what we're receiving. The only way to accept your self is to accept God.

LOVE

Love can make you feel different, look different and act different.

Love can make you smile, cry and laugh all at once.

Love can make you dream big, strive to be more successful,

and live your life for the one you love.

We do all these things for our earthly love.

But the question is what, do we do for our real love,

our true love, our eternal love.

It Is The Greatest Of All Loves!

Once you possess this love there is no turning back. Once you have experienced this love, no man, no woman, no earthly being will ever be good enough. The love I'm talking about is God's love.

When you have experienced this love you feel joy because

you know just how good it is! It's fulfilling, exciting, unconditional, and it doesn't require much of you, all you have to do is love and respect God with your heart and soul!

God's love is the image we need to mirror our lives and earthly loves after.

We need to ask God to come into our lives, and to send

us the man or woman that God has chosen for us.

Love should not be hard, nor should it be complicated,

it should not hurt nor should it cause pain.

Love should be like taking a drink of water on the hottest day of the year,

it should quench your thirst ......

Satisfy you, that you may thirst no more.

That is how I feel when the Holy Spirit stops by to remind me of the love that God has for me!

LOVE ...

Love is an awesome experience, but if you don't have the love of God in your heart you will never be able to experience true love in the earth.

That Love

I miss **That Love** that I thought I once knew.

I miss **That Love** that is pure and true.

I miss **That Love** that I dream of,
That Love that God has for me.

It is real, honest, strong, and pure. It's not jealous, it doesn't hurt, cost, and it doesn't flirt. It's real, true, exciting and unique. There is no one like it; you can't get it any and everywhere. You must be patient, ready, careful, and carefree. You must enjoy it, but not indulge, you must accept it and honor it, and you must treasure it and keep it sacred. Once you experience it you must rejoice in it!

How will you know when you find it? You will walk, talk and feel different but more importantly, you will love different. When God has blessed you with **That Love** you will know!

That Love ...

God has a special love that he has for each one of us. It is a Love that is pure and unique, designed just for each of us. Just ask God to direct you to the person he has for you. Put it all in his hands and he will send you your soul mate!

I am of You and You are in Me

I am of you and you are in me.

As I think of all that I have done and all that I will some day achieve, I imagine where I would be if you were not in me.

I thank you for blessing me and sending so many my way.

At the moment I may not have understood what they were saying to me, but everyone you placed in my life that spoke your name I shall never forget.

They may not realize the impact of what they were saying, but no matter who it was when you speak the word of God I hear.

Everyone I have met along the way has not always meant me good, but God has a way of removing people like that from your life and I am very grateful.

As their words may have saved me or reminded me of your grace and mercy my words may have been the saving grace they needed!

You have blessed me with such an amazing gift that I pray you will continue to use me, lead and direct me that I may continue to do your will!

If I could show one, only one to God, then I shall
Be satisfied. But if I can lead a whole flock
To him, then my soul may be at rest!

I am of You and You are in Me ...

You are my protector and my right hand and I am blessed that you are in me. I spend my days thanking you for choosing me to be a part of you and for living in me. You manifest in many, but only few accept you ... thank you for your patience.

When God Stops By

As I lie in my bed and wonder should I watch TV, should I read or should I write? I begin to think about all that I've been through, seen, and experienced. I begin to pray and write and write and pray. I am not pausing; I am not thinking, nor contemplating the words I should use. And then I stop... I hear something. It's not loud or deep, it's a still small voice like a whisper... my body gets warm, my eyes begin to water and my hand begins to write again and when I am done I smile, because I know that it was God stopping by for just a little while. I take a deep breath and take it all in and thank him again for choosing me!

When God Stops By ...

The feeling I get when God stops by is at times explainable but unexplainable for many. People who don't know or have a personal relationship with God can't understand how someone could feel that way when you haven't seen him, but when you know who God is you're excited to hear another person testify of their experience. Put your faith in him and experience God stopping by.

Forever Thanking You

I give you thanks and the praise!

Your mercy and grace is amazing!

You have allowed me to do so many things and accomplish
so many goals and for that I am thanking you!

You woke me up when you could have let me rest forever!

You fed me when I could have gone hungry forever!

You blessed me when you could have made me suffer forever
and for that I'm forever thanking you!

I love, praise, thank and worship you!

My life is not what you would have it to be, but I am thanking
you that it is not nearly what it used to be!

And for that alone I am Forever Thanking You!

Forever Thanking You …

I wanted to end with this poem because it is the gratitude that I feel for God all in one. He has been so many things to me over the years and I am forever grateful. I know I have a ways to go on my Christian journey, but as long as I have God with me there is nothing I cannot do. And for that I am Forever Thanking You!

Prayers from my Soul

Heavenly Father I come to you in prayer humbly thanking and praising you for all you've done and all you will do. I thank you for waking me up this morning, placing your hands upon me that I may do your will on this day and the days to come. Heavenly Father I thank you for seeing something special in me. I pray that I may do your will here on earth and spend forever with you. You have continued to lead and guide me throughout all of my mistakes, and my short comings. You've stayed with me and I thank you because without you I have nothing and I am nothing. This is my prayer in Jesus name…Amen!

Heavenly Father I would like to give honor to God. I would like to thank you for all the blessings you have bestowed upon me. I'd like to thank you for allowing me to see my children another day. Thank you for my family and their spiritual foundation and the spiritual guidance you give me. Thank you for choosing me. I am so overjoyed that I am able to write about the greatness of the Lord and all that he is able to do. Thank you for showing me my talents and my gifts. Thank you for your constant words of encouragement and for placing in me what you would have for me to give to your children. Thank you for allowing the visions you gave to me years ago to come to pass in your time. I am truly blessed and I pray that you will continue to speak to me and allow me to speak of your mercy and to tell my story. I pray that someone will be saved by the words that you have placed on my tongue. In Jesus name I pray...Amen

Heavenly Father as I think of the goodness and the greatness of the Lord I think of the praise that we give you. Heavenly Father we praise you for all the things you do for us big and small. We praise you for the difference you've made within us, and we thank you for all that you have done and all that you will do. Heavenly Father as we praise you we are either calling out for your deliverance or thanking you for already delivering us. Even though we may not say it each time, but the praise and the thankfulness we give you is our plea for deliverance. We are praying for deliverance from sin, drugs, alcohol, abuse, promiscuity, all other addictions and anything that is not of God. Heavenly Father I just pray that you will find me pleasing in your sight! Amen!

Heavenly Father I come to you in prayer. I am thanking you for all you are doing in my life. Things have not always been easy and the road hasn't always been straight. There were times in my life when I wasn't sure when the tears would stop falling or how I would be brought out of my misery, but I thank you because you allowed me to see there was more to life. Because of your faithfulness to your child I have been set free. The burden of the world, the burden of leaning on my own understanding has been lifted and I now walk taller, I smile bigger, and my testimony is more meaningful. I now understand that in order to reap all of your benefits I had to have joy even when I don't want to. Heavenly Father I thank you and I praise you in Jesus name...Amen!

Heavenly Father I come to you thanking you for all you have done with my life. You have sheltered me from the cold of the world and you have quenched my thirst with your word. Heavenly Father all that I am is because of you and all that I desire to be is because of the example of eternal life that I may have! There is a fire that burns inside of me, a fire that makes me want to shout because of the goodness of the Lord! You have placed something inside of me that often cannot be contained, that is unexplainable, and incomparable, you are like no other and I thank you for everything! In Jesus Name…Amen!

Poems and Prayers from your Soul

I wanted to add a section that allows you, the reader to express yourself. A place that allows you to reflect on your life, your experiences, obstacles that you have been delivered from or just blessings. A place that you can look back on and reflect to see where you have been in your life and to remind you of where you are headed. I pray that this section will be as special to you as my poems and prayers are to me, because I believe there is strength and power in expressing yourself through words! Enjoy and be blessed!

Message To The Reader:

Always, pray your own prayer.

God hears all and he heals all who have faith in Him!

www.ingramcontent.com/pod-product-compliance
Lightning Source LLC
Chambersburg PA
CBHW031904170626
46807CB00004B/1890